Scripture And Coloring

Inspirational Coloring Book For Girls

Simone Gillespie

Dear children, let us not love with words or speech but with actions and in truth.

1 John 3:18

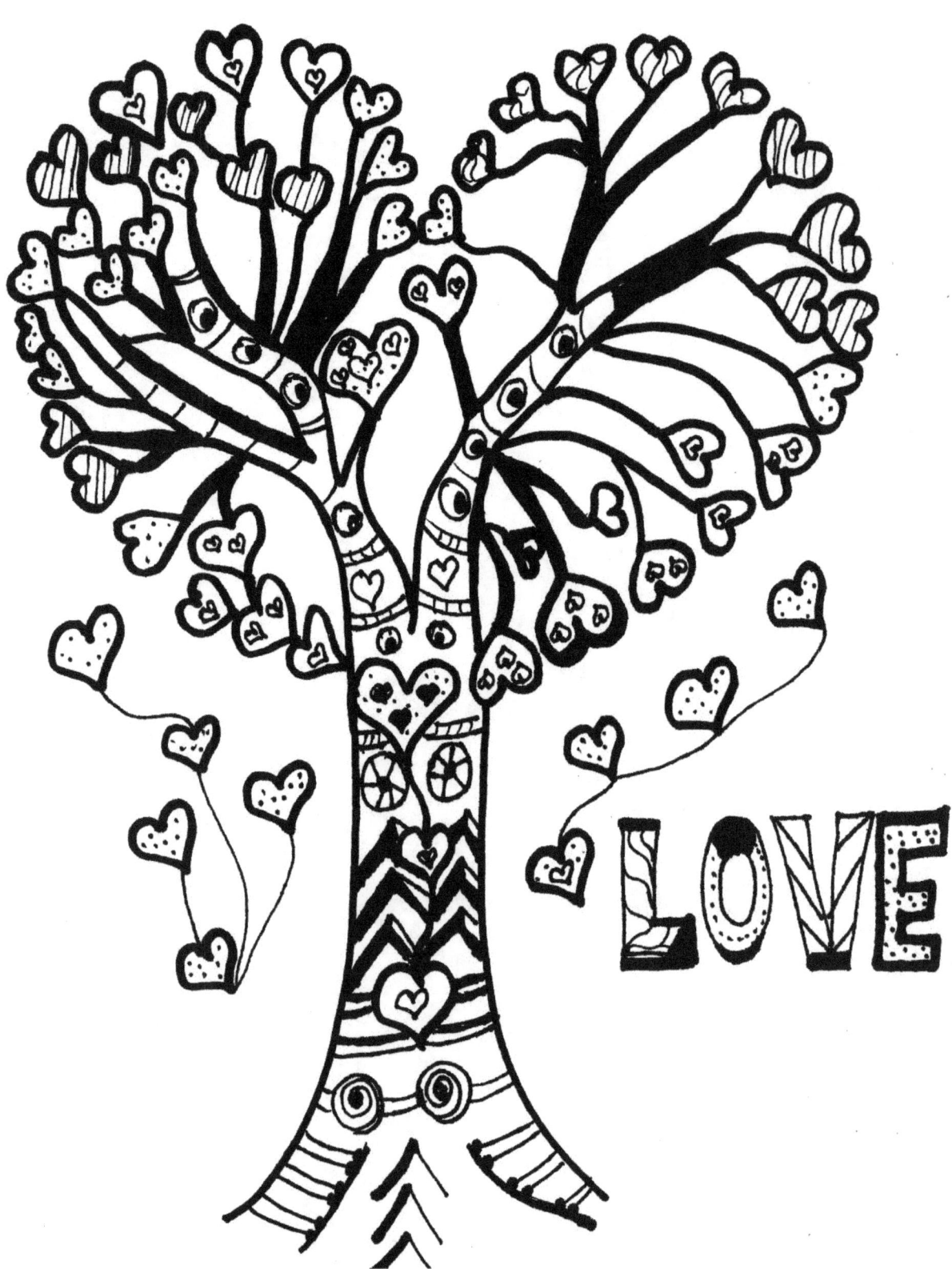

Do what is honest.

2 Corinthians 13:7

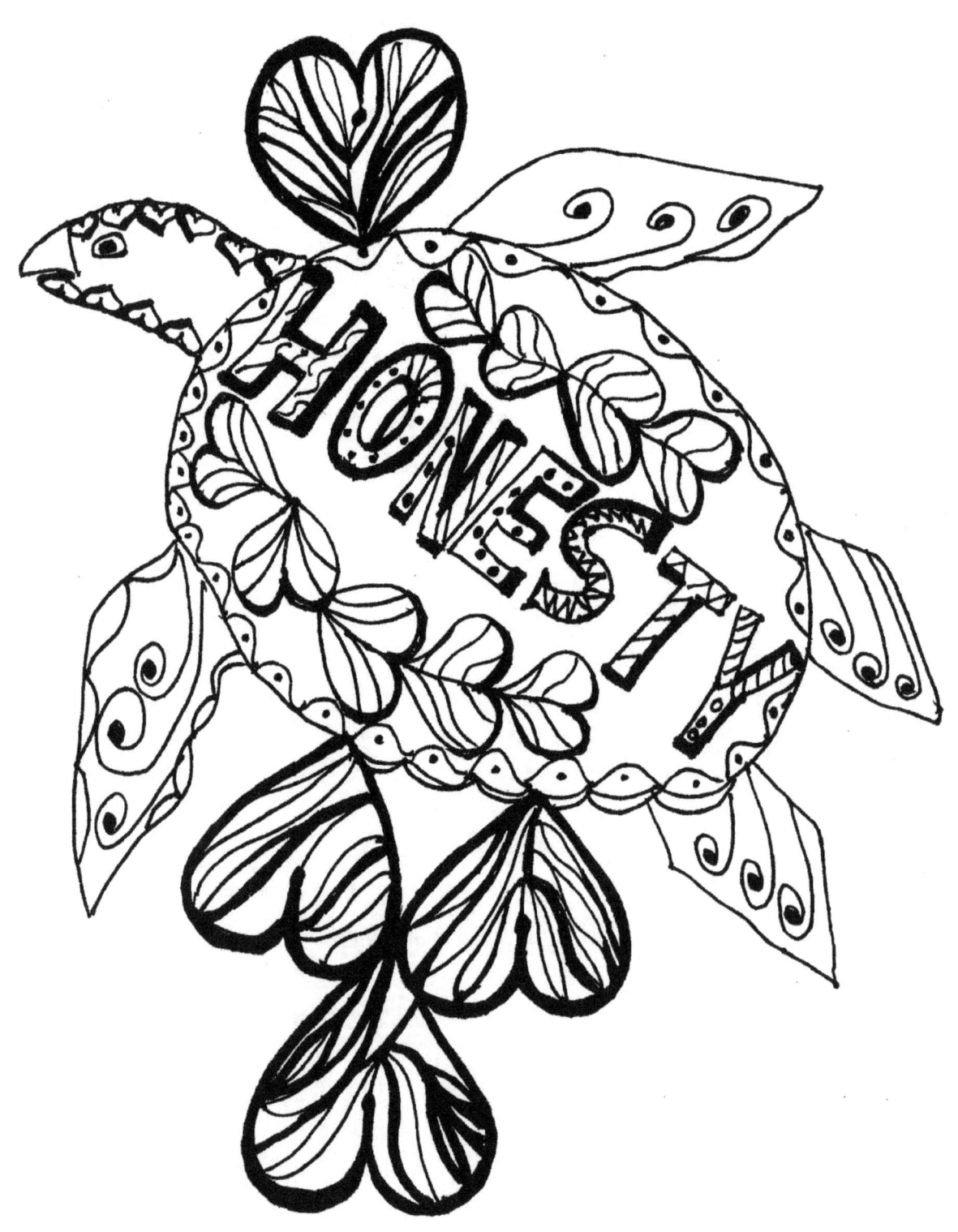

The Lord our God is merciful and forgiving.

Daniel 9:9

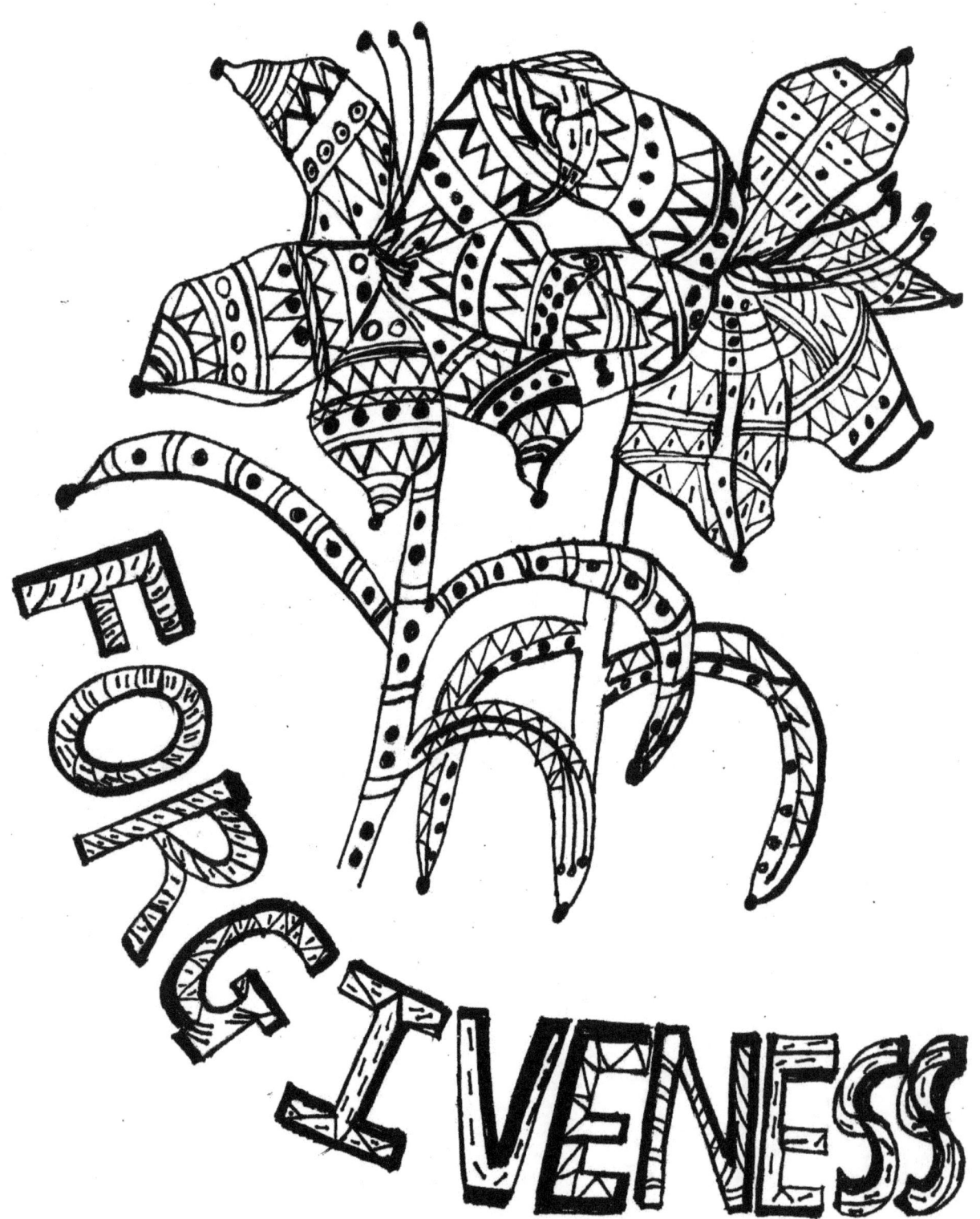

Your word is a lamp for my feet and a light on my path.

Psalm 119:105

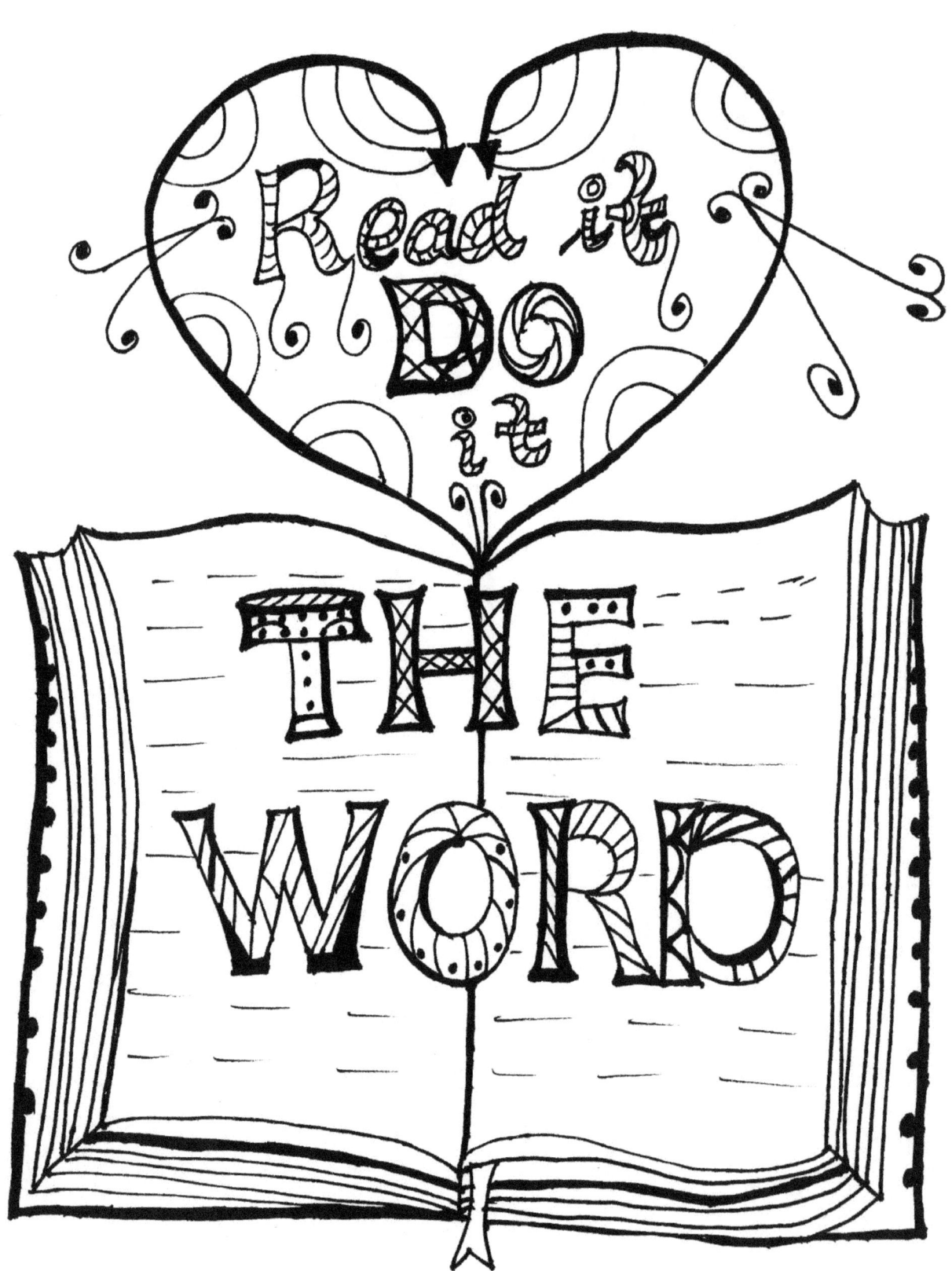

"With everlasting kindness I will have compassion on you," says the LORD your Redeemer.

Isiah 54:8

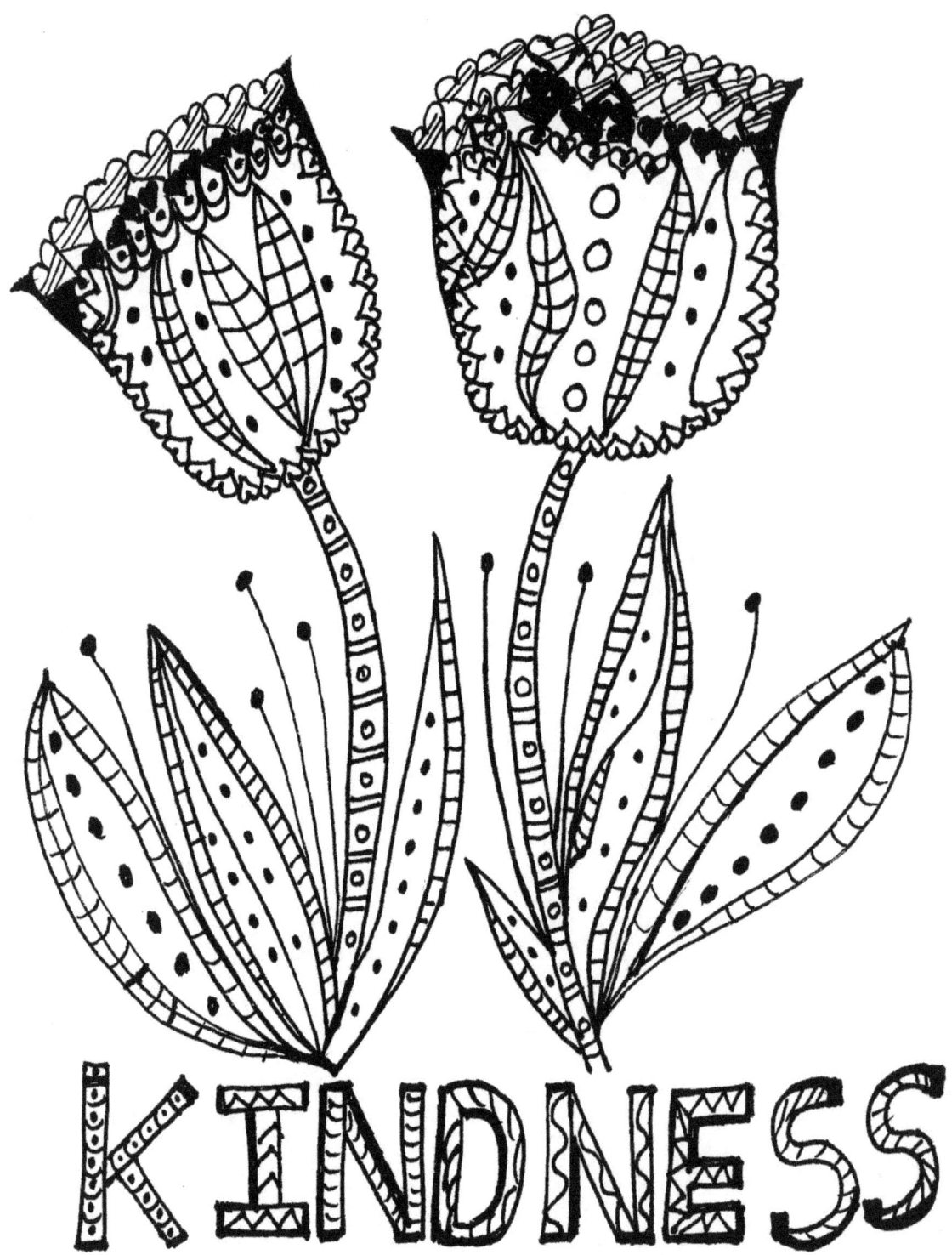

In everything give thanks.

1 Thessalonians 5:18

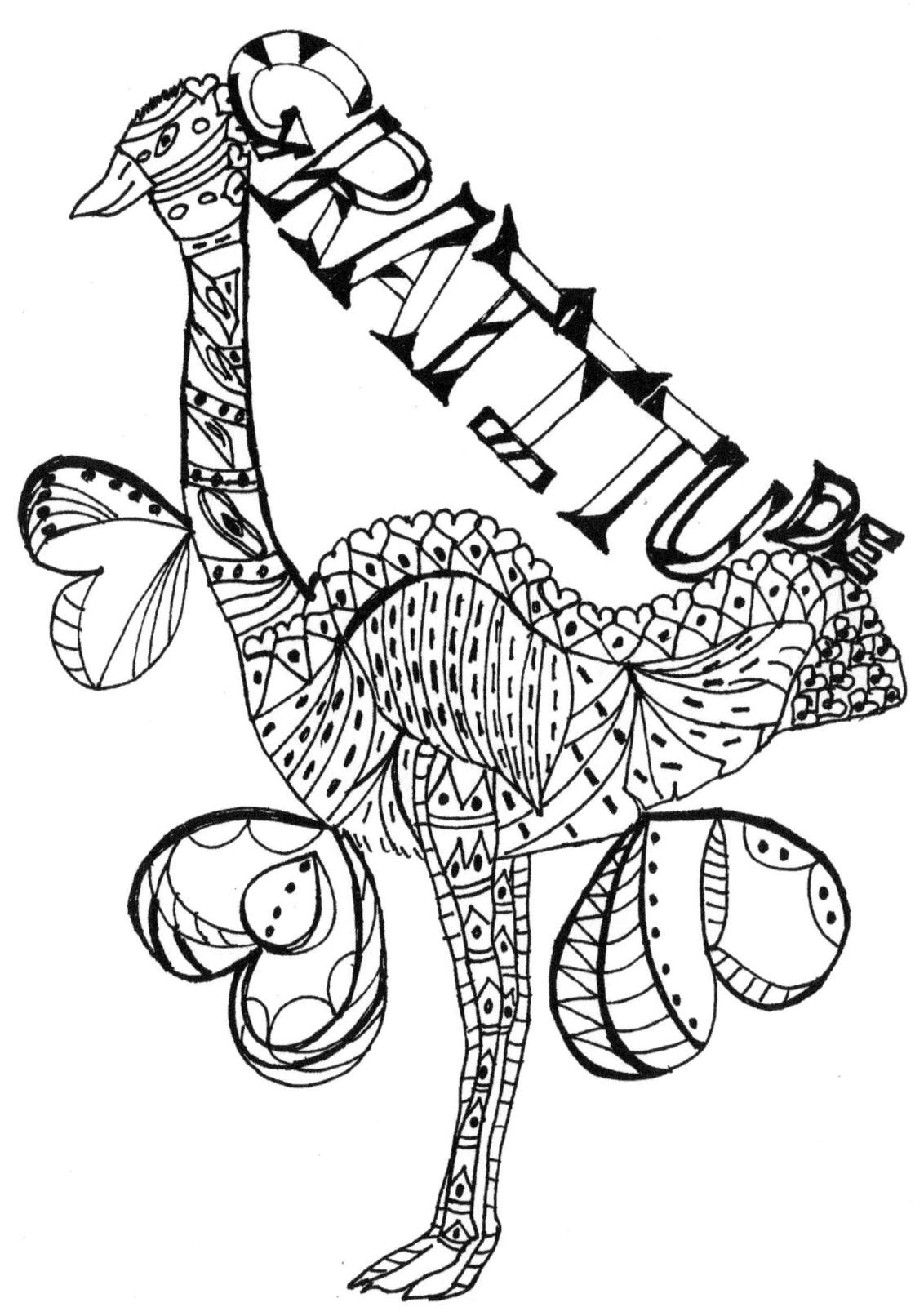

How much better to get wisdom than gold.

Proverbs 16:16

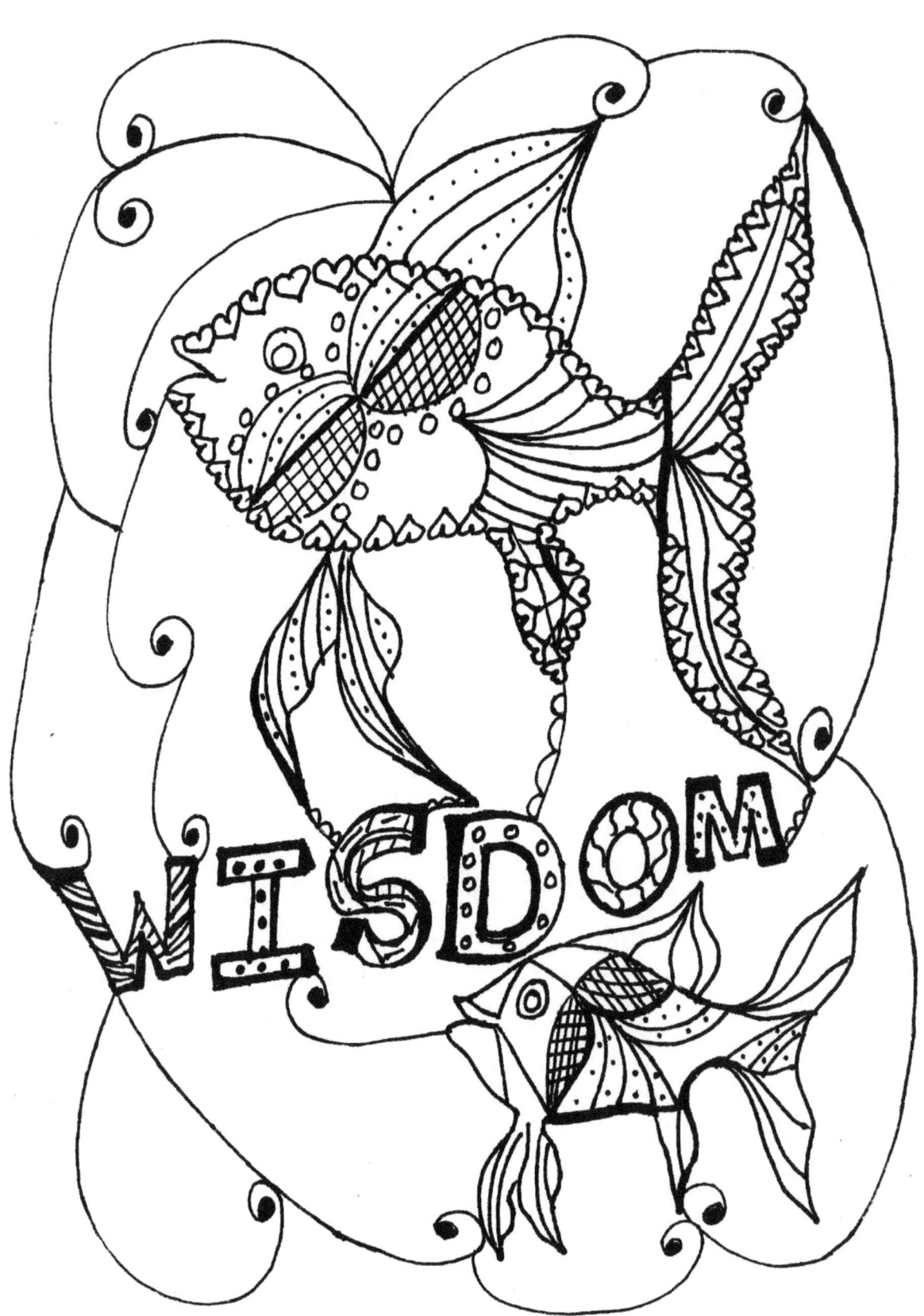

Each of you must respect his mother and his father.

Leviticus 19:3

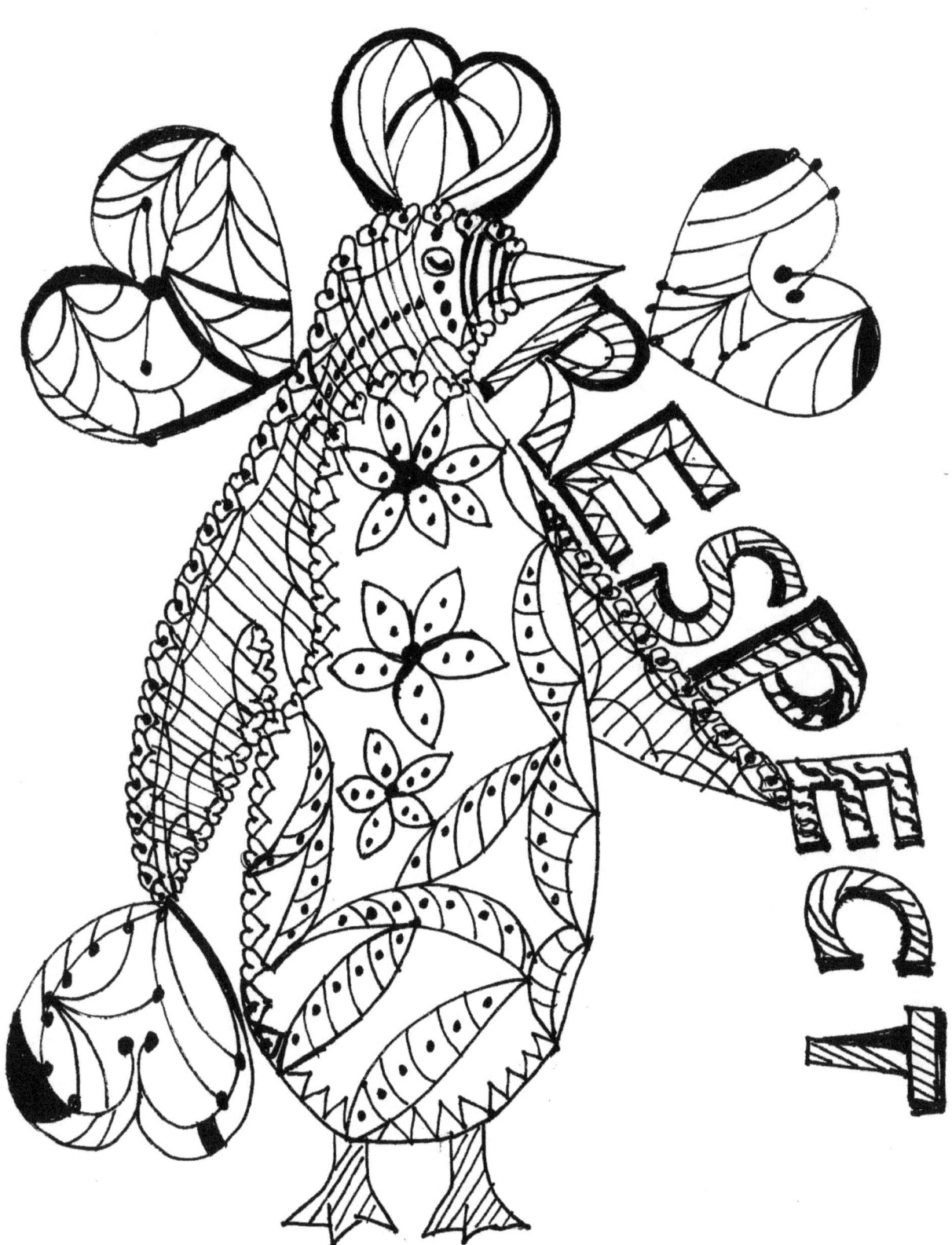

The lazy person craves, yet receives nothing, but the desires of the diligent are satisfied.

Proverbs 13:4

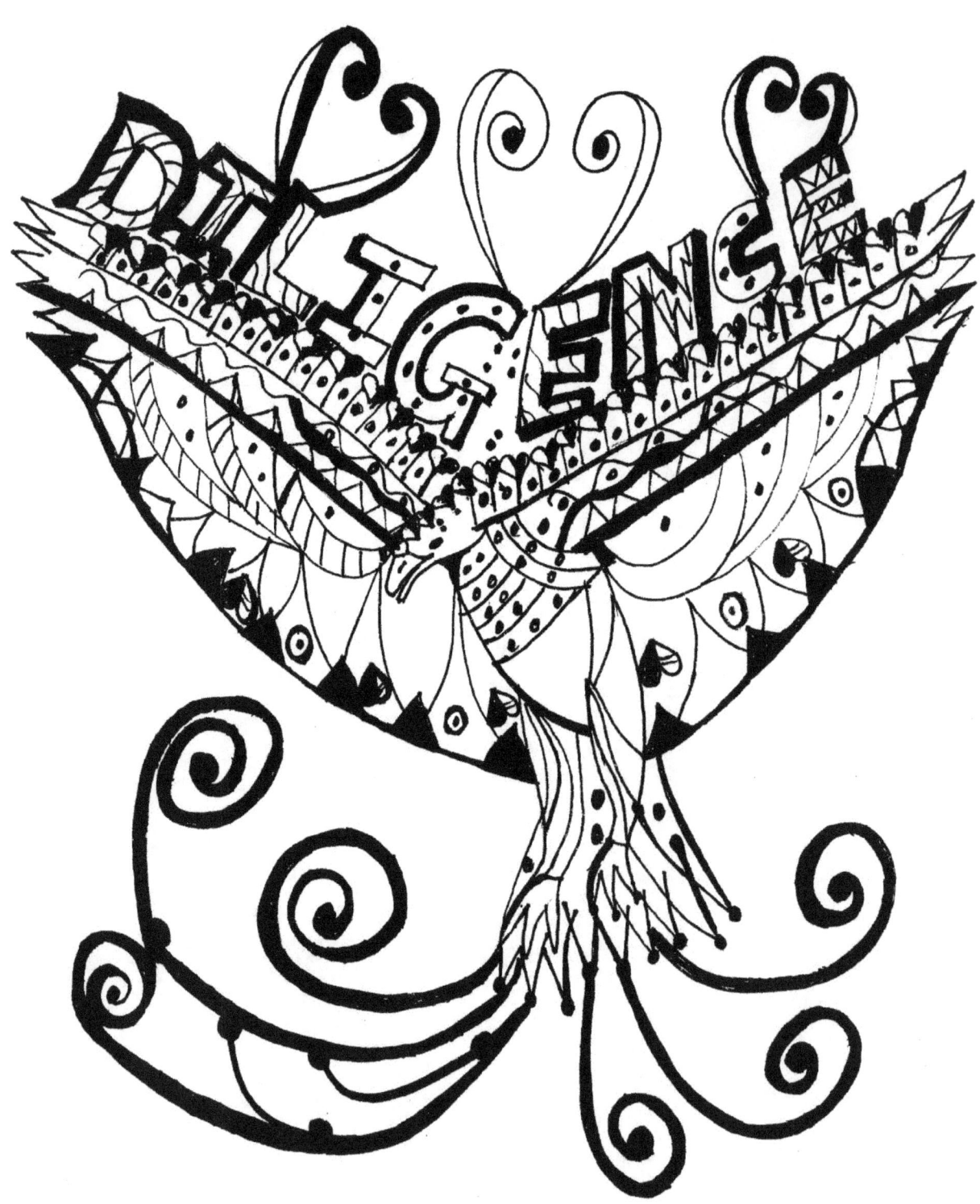

Each of you must take responsibility for doing the best you can with your life.

Galations 6:5

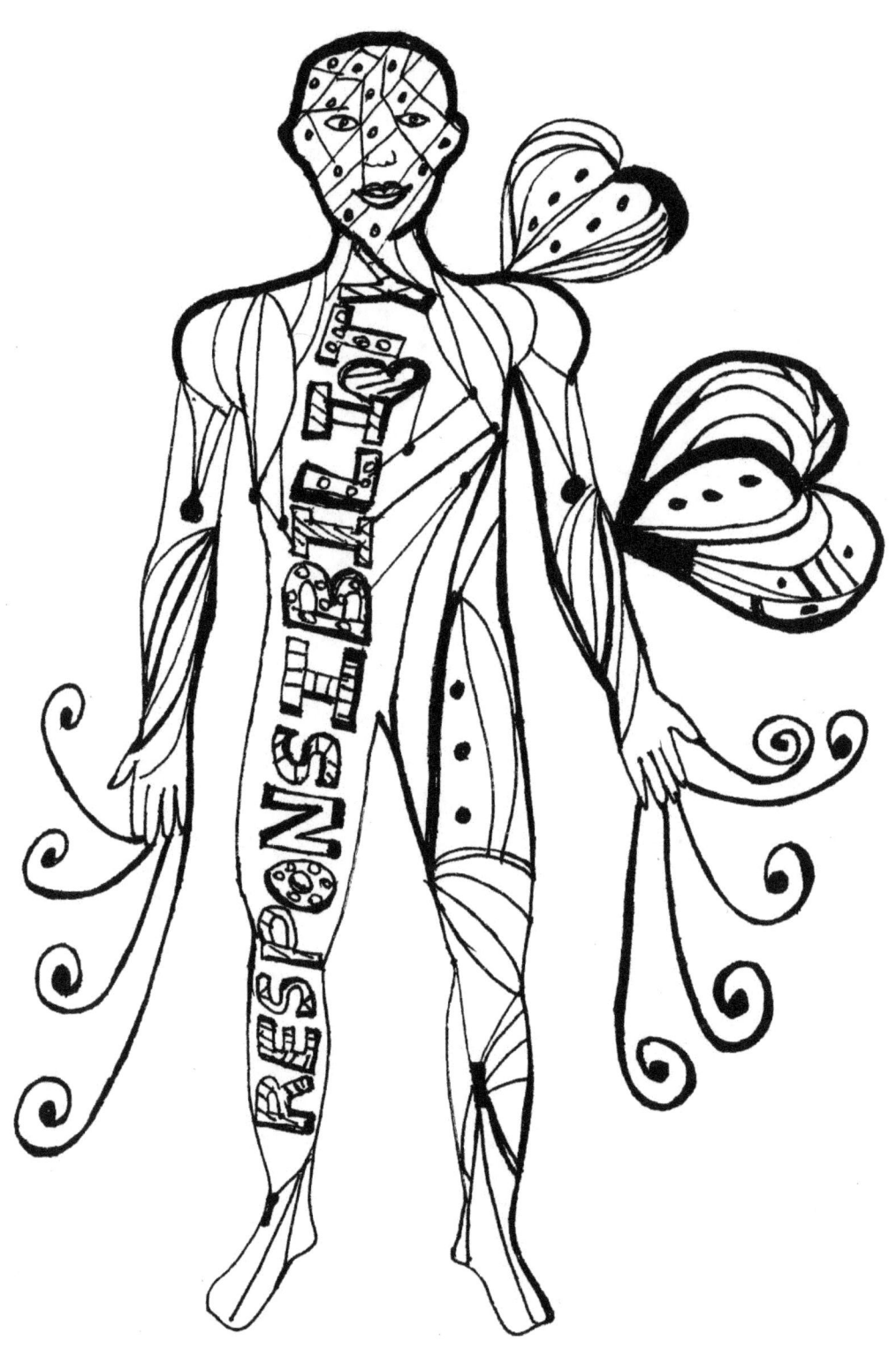

May the God of hope
fill you with all joy and
peace.

Romans 15:13

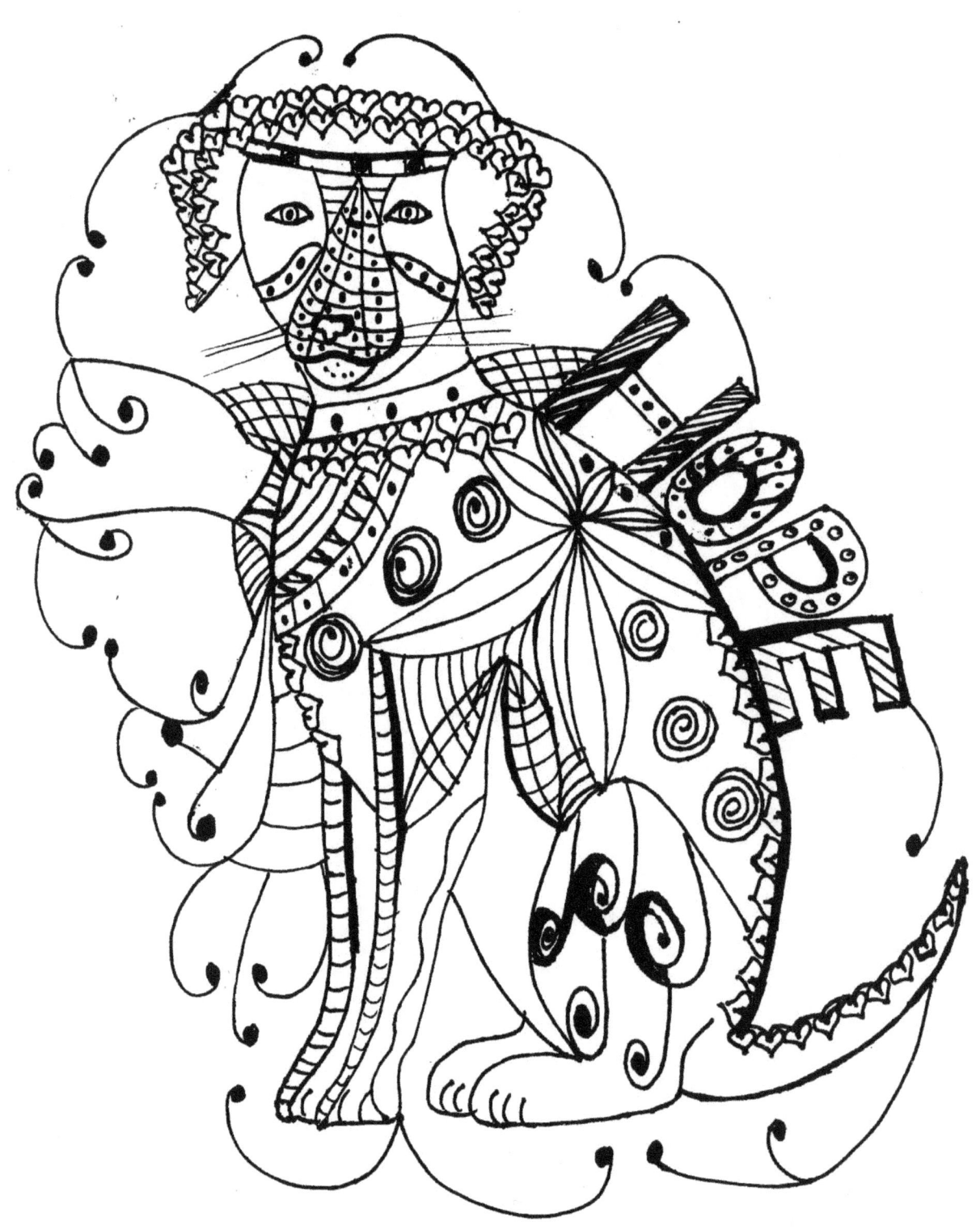

Without faith it is impossible to please God.

Hebrews 16:6

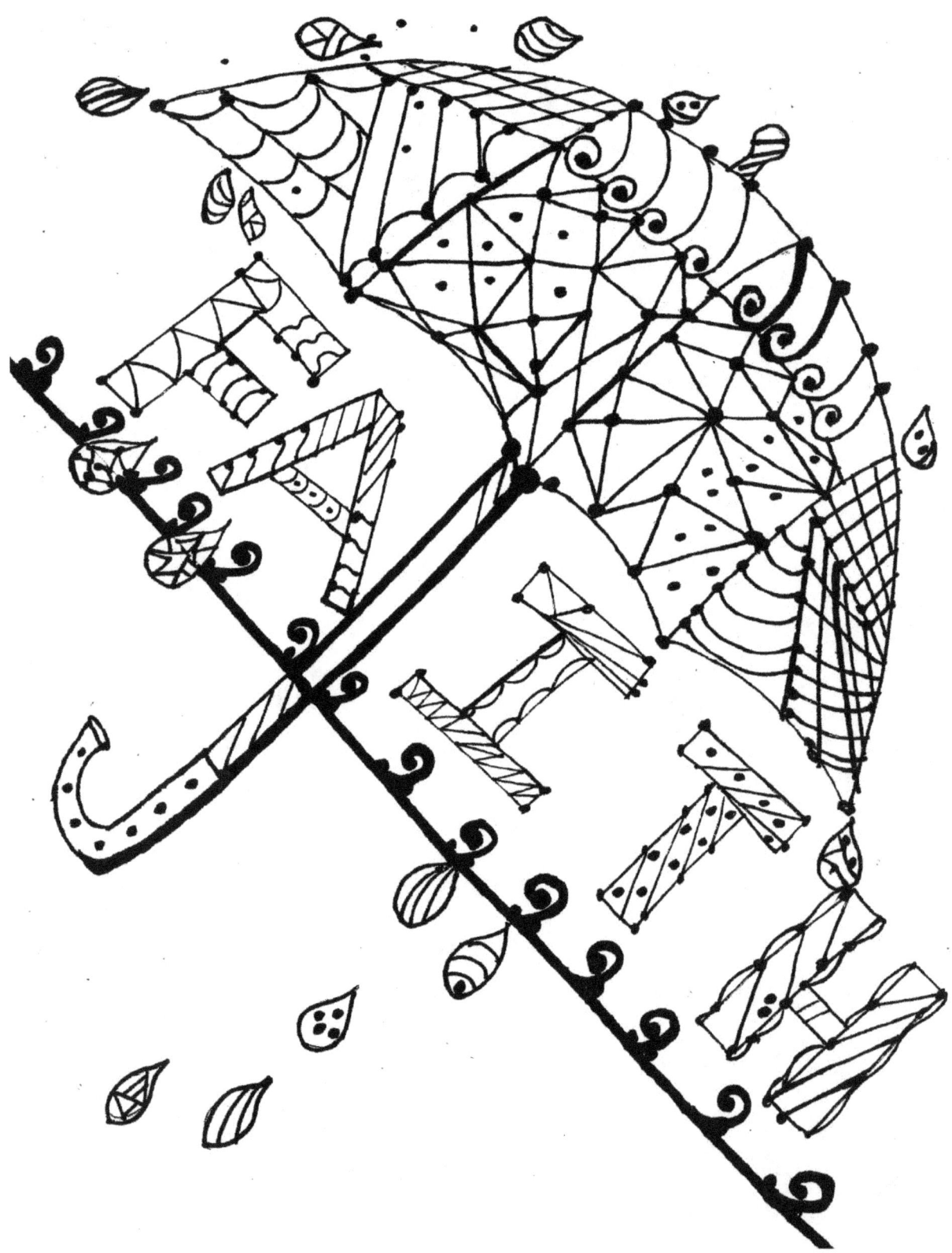

Blessed are the peacemakers, for they will be called children of God.

Matthew 5:9

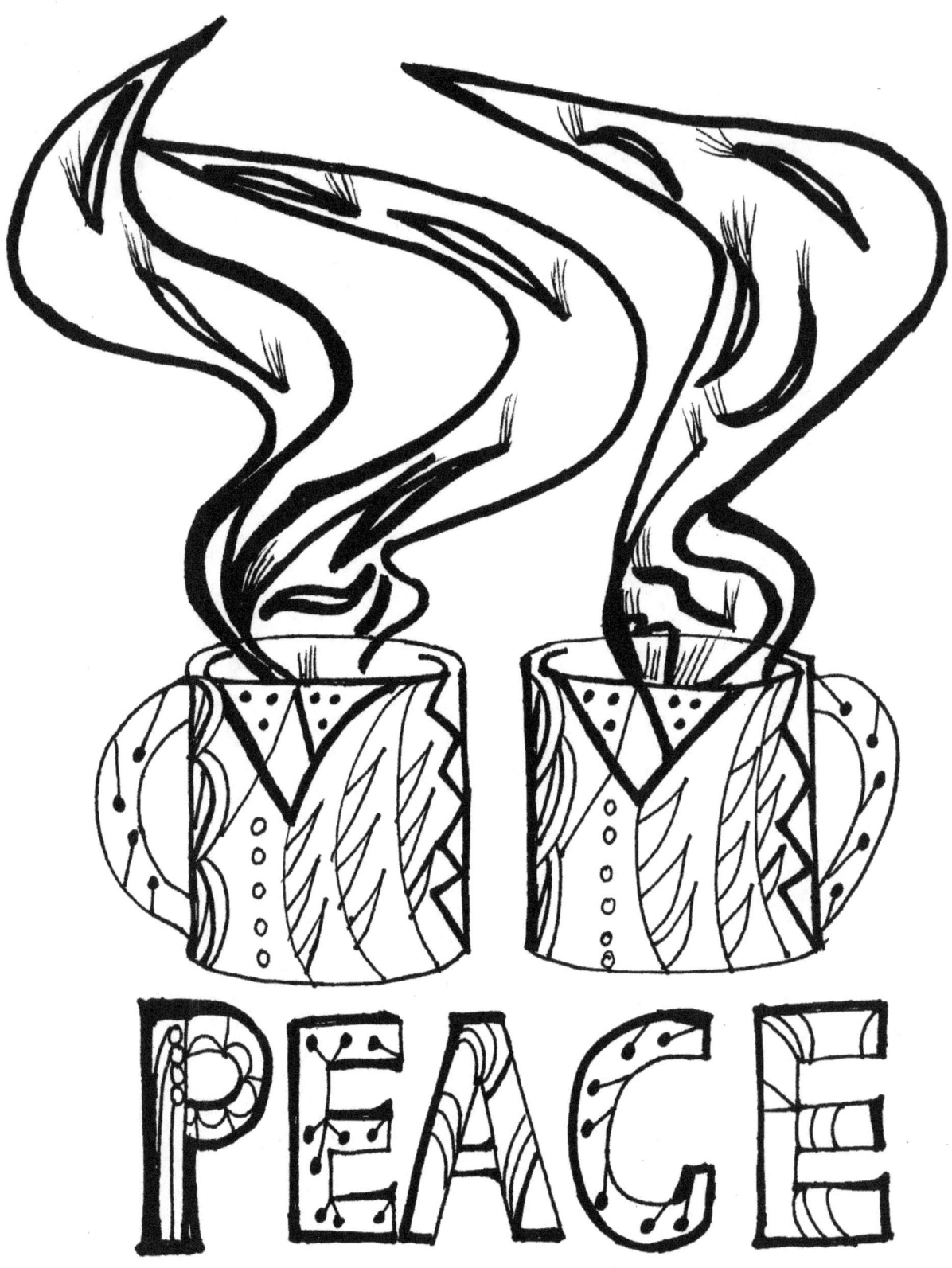

The Lord will guide you continually.

Isiah 58:11

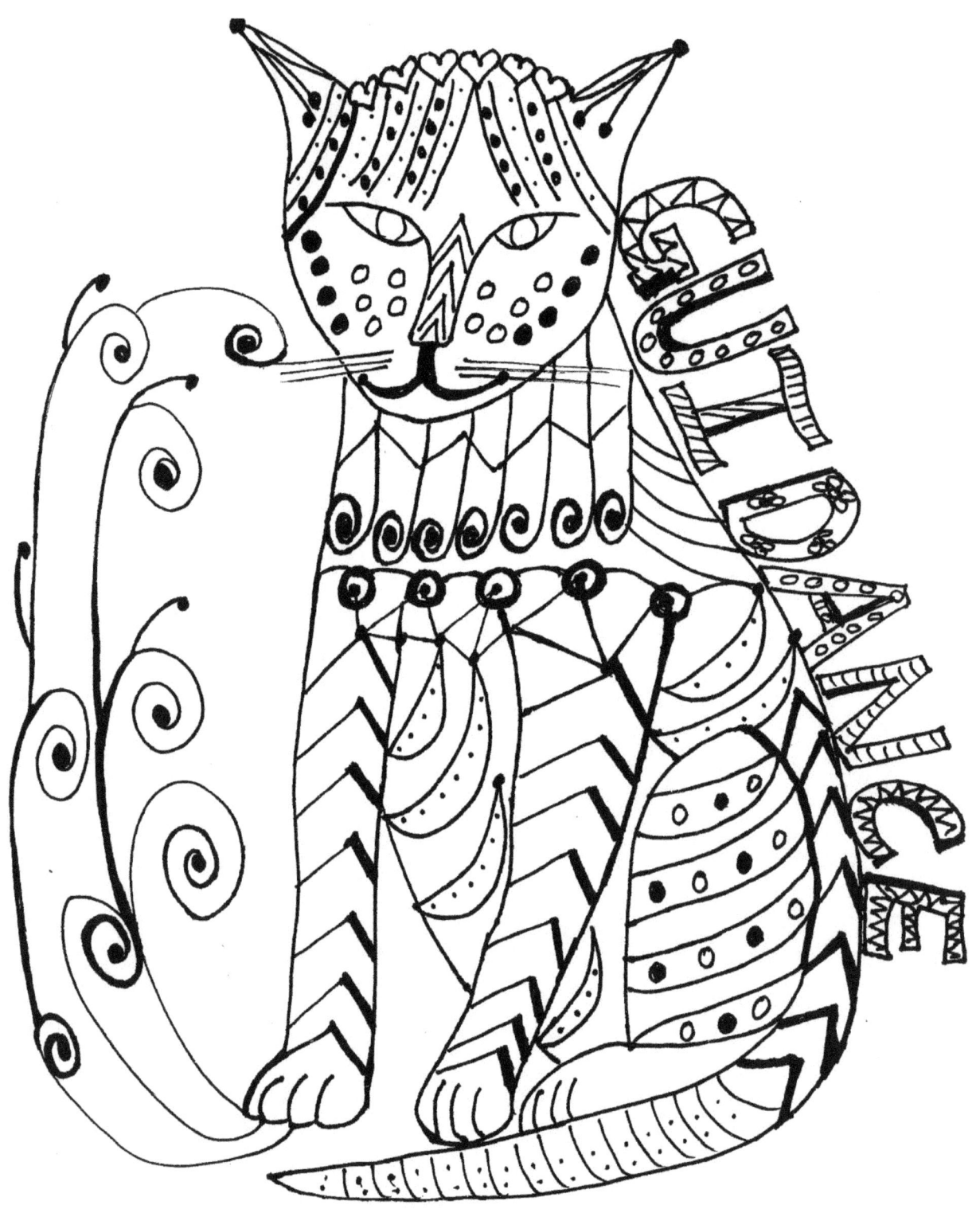

Blessed are those who persevere under trial.

James 1:12

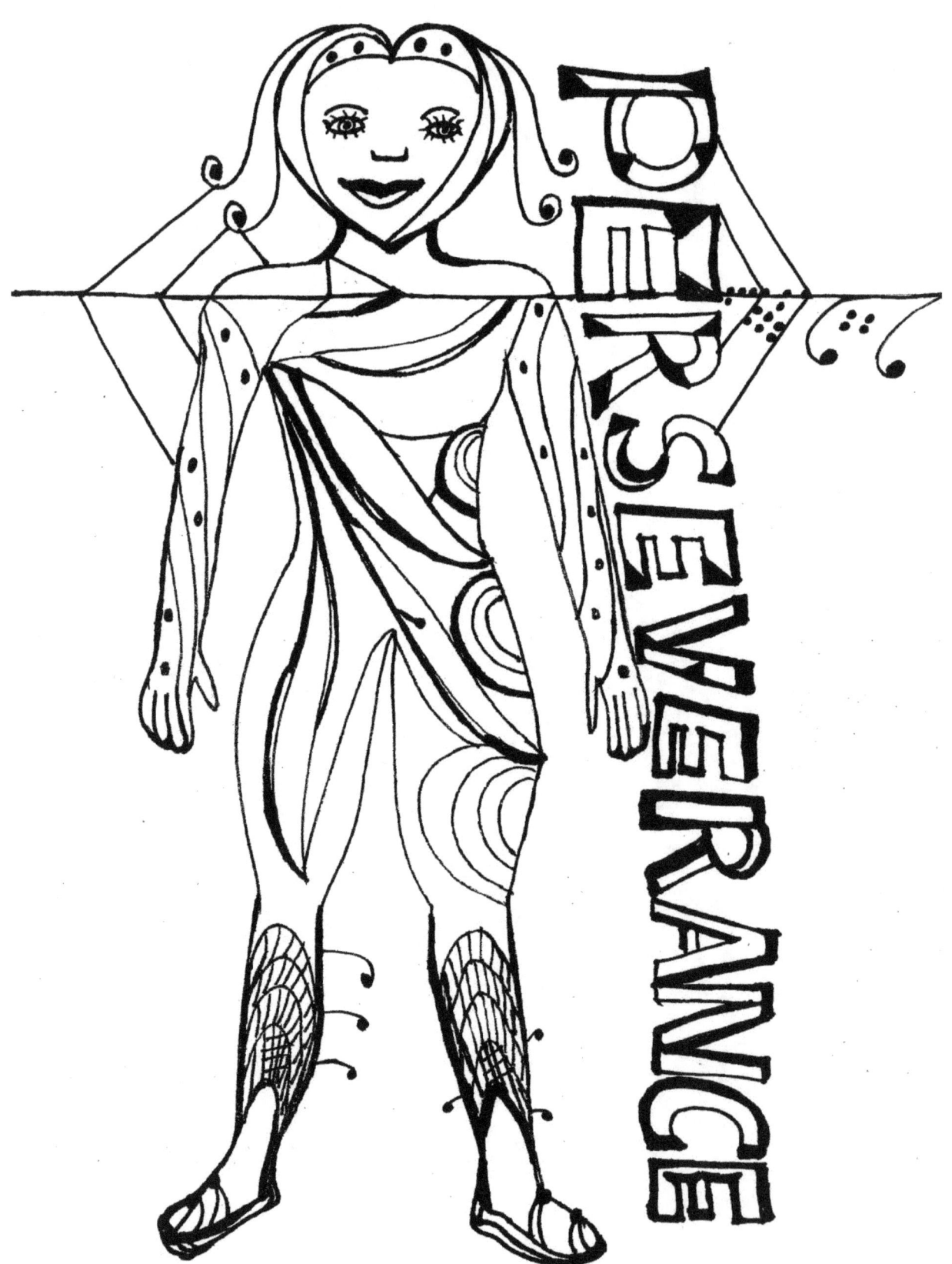

For it is by grace you have been saved.

Ephesians 2:8

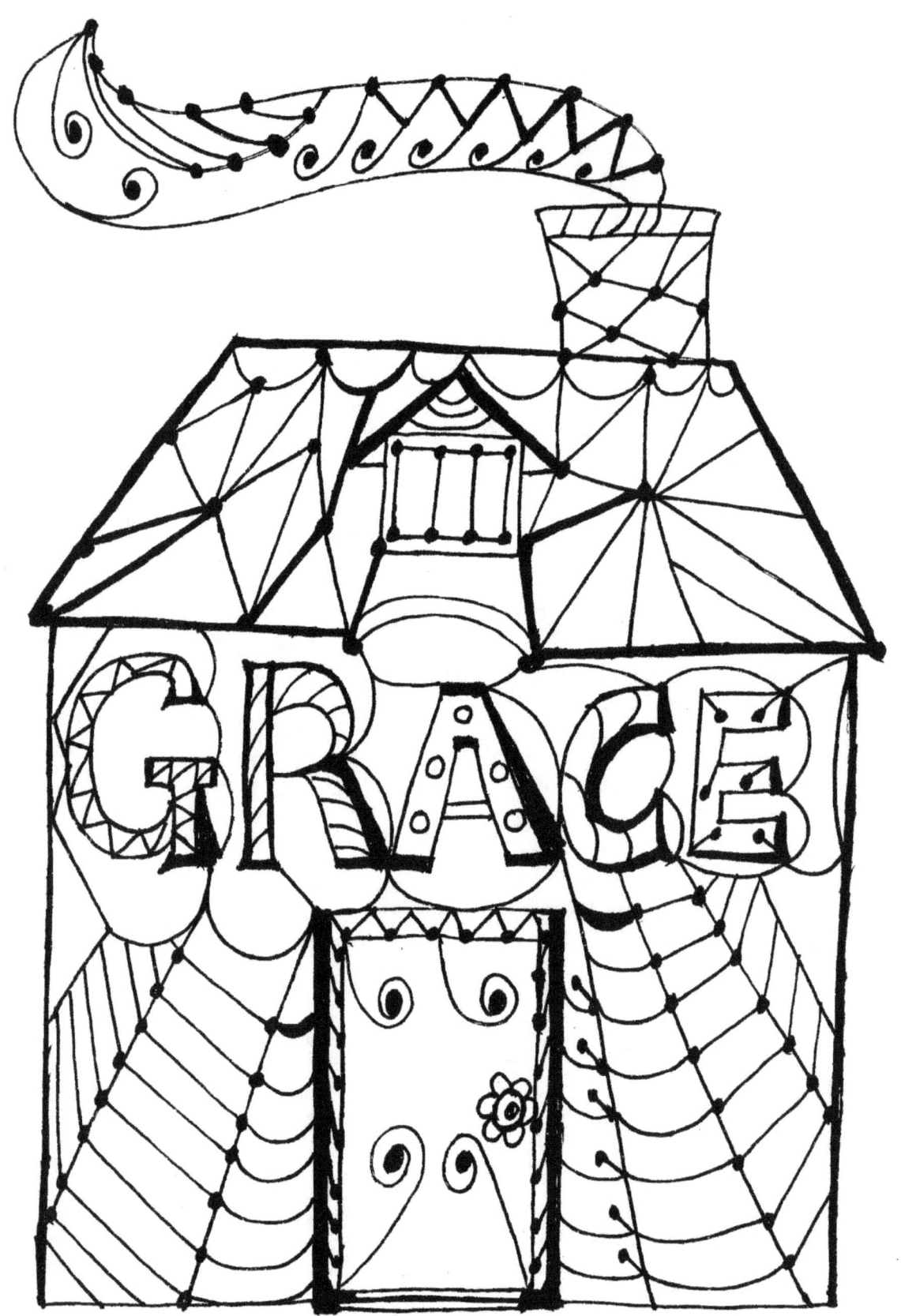

God, who is rich in mercy, made us alive with Christ even when we were dead in sin.

<u>Ephesians 2:4</u>

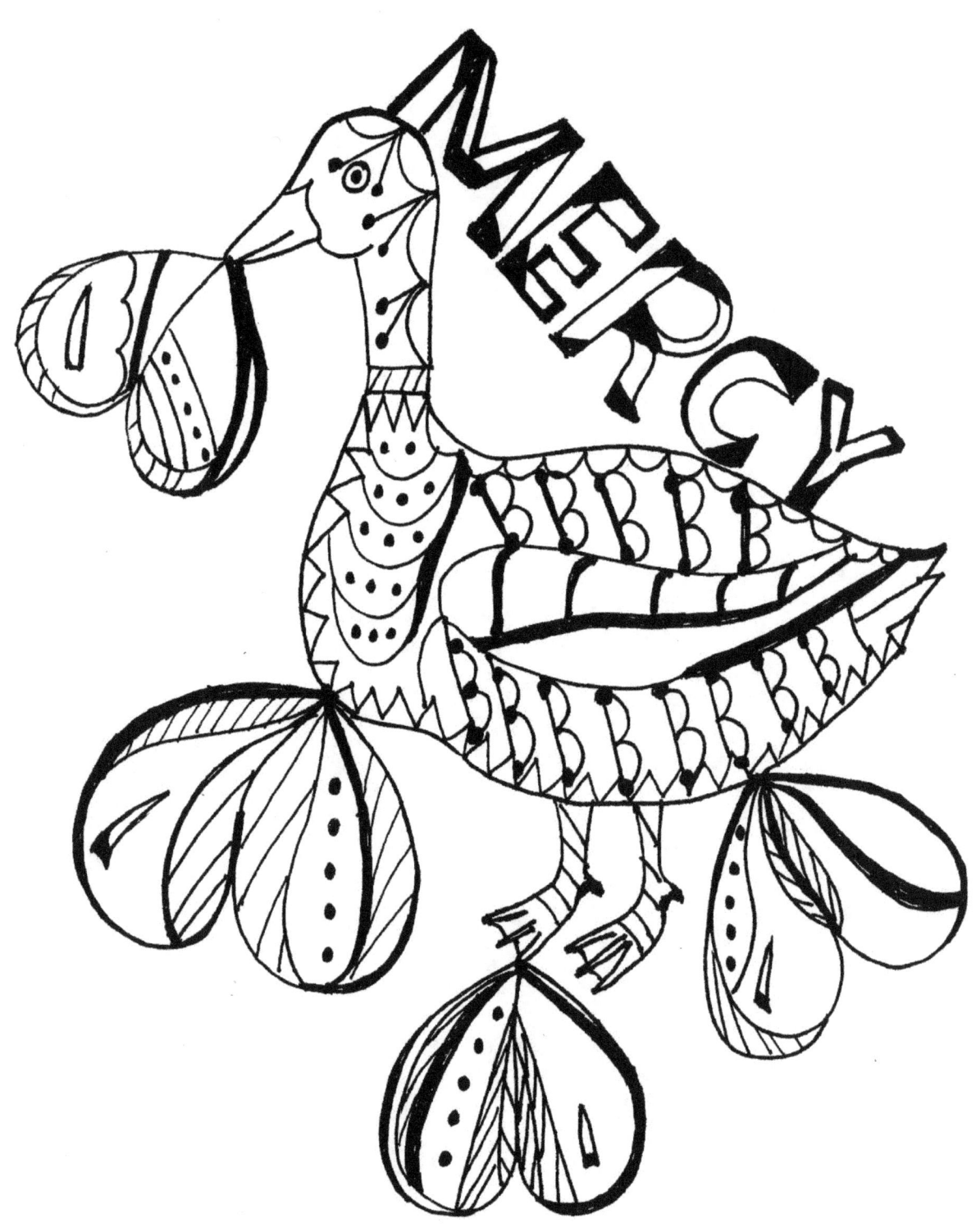

Be of good courage,
and God will strengthen
your heart.

Psalm 31:24

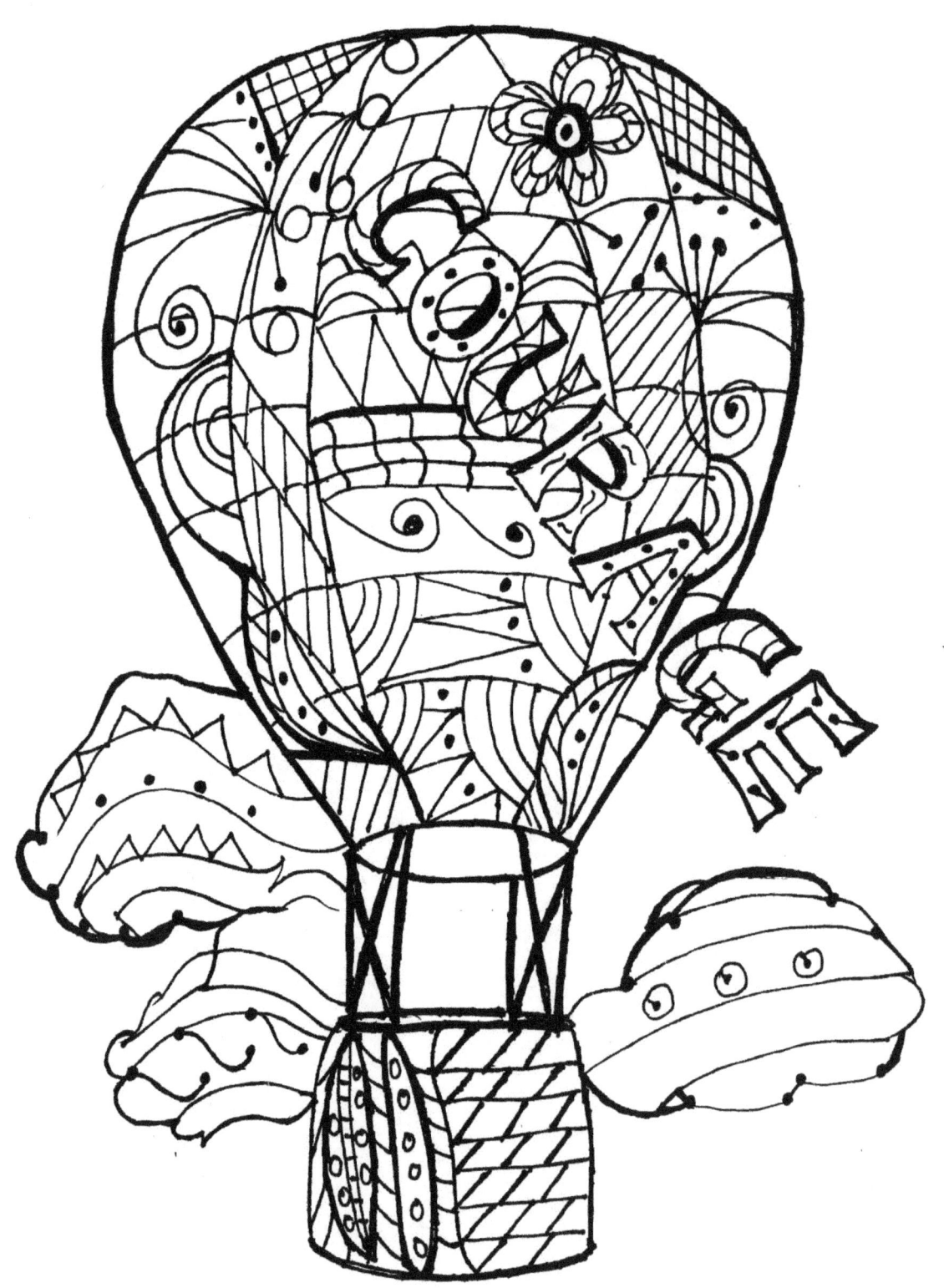

Each one should use whatever gift he has received to serve others.

1 Peter 4:10

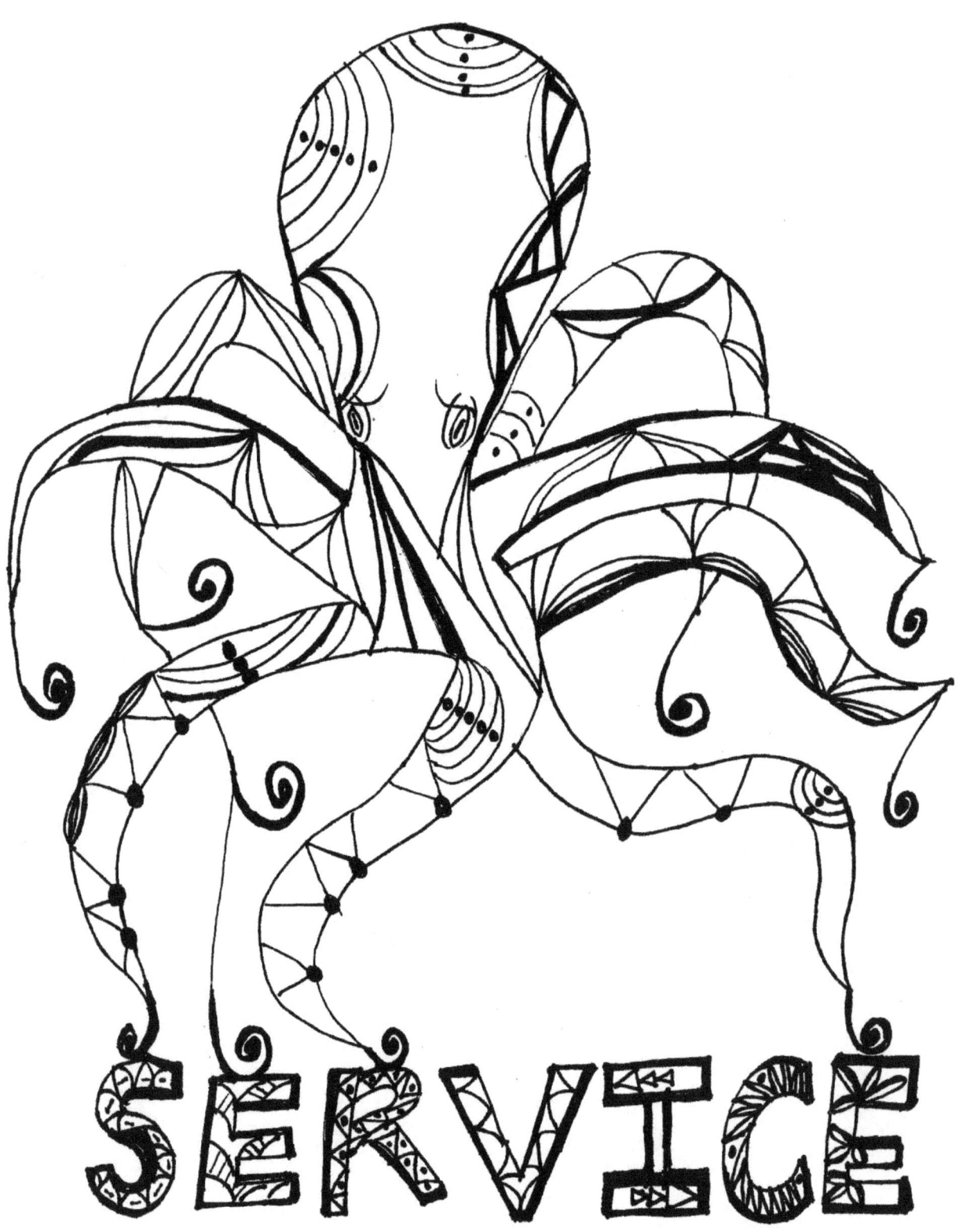

Beloved, I wish above all things that you may prosper.

3 John 1:3

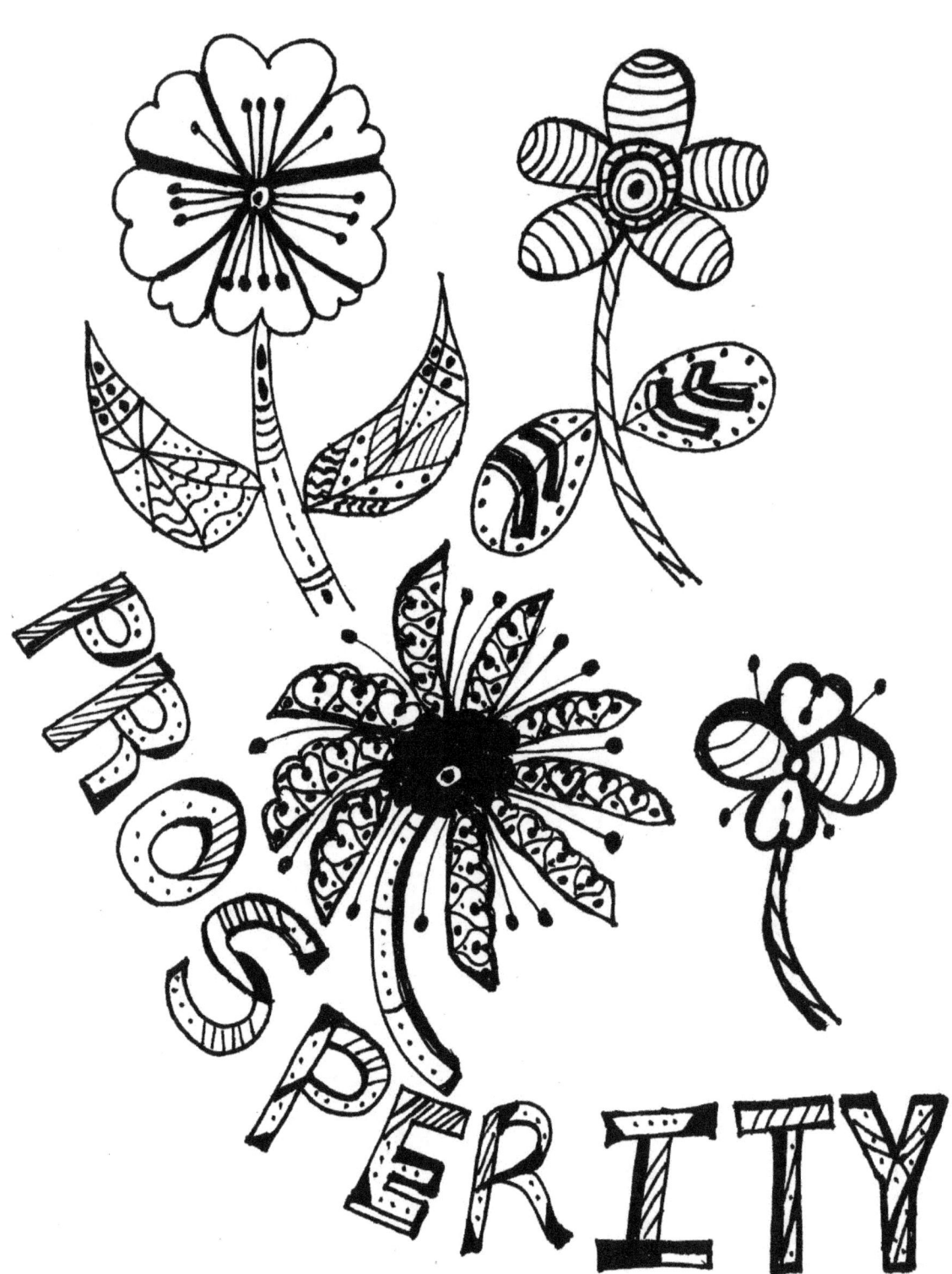

For You, O Lord, will bless the righteous with favor.

Psalm 5:12

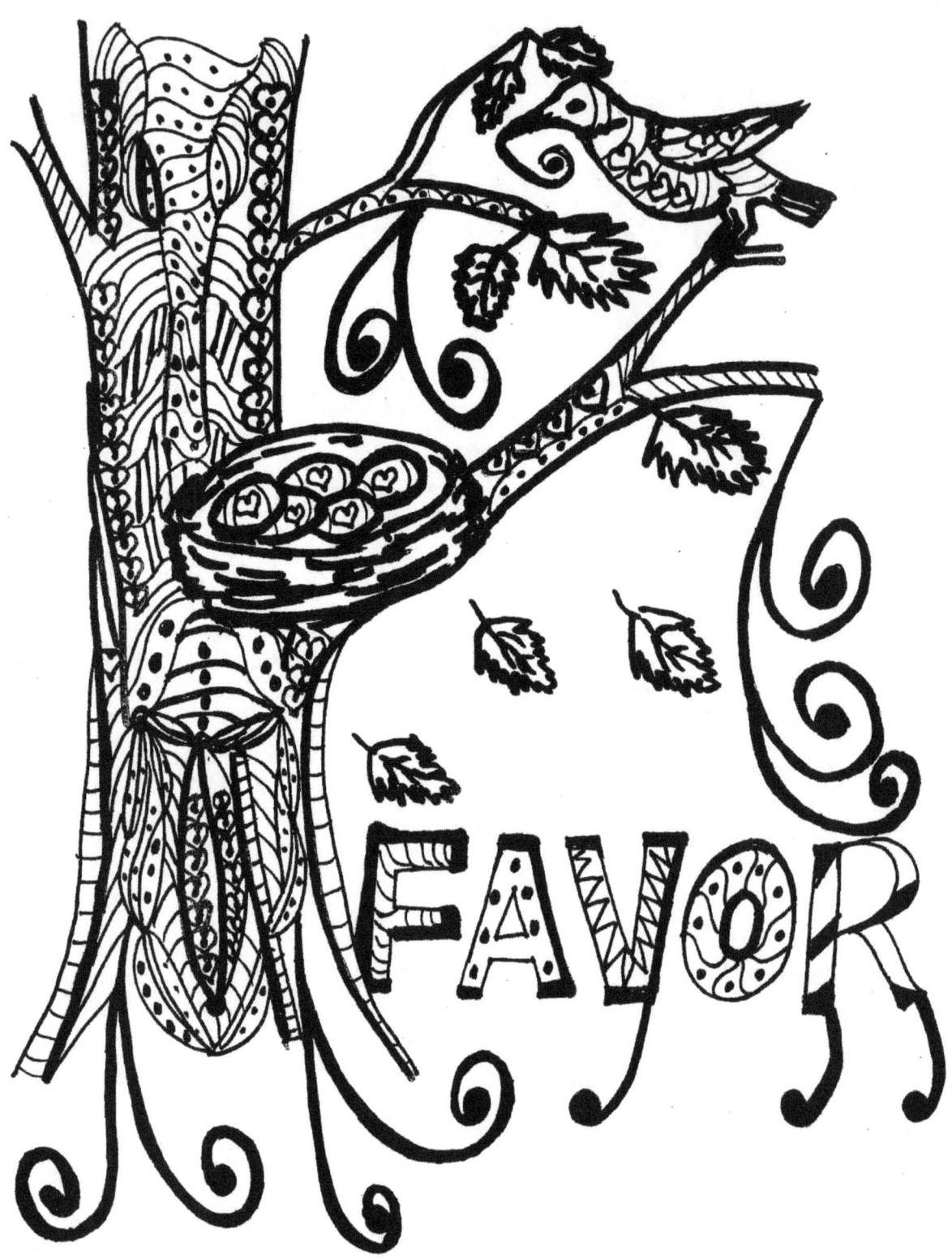

Be still before the Lord and wait patiently for him.

Psalm 37:7

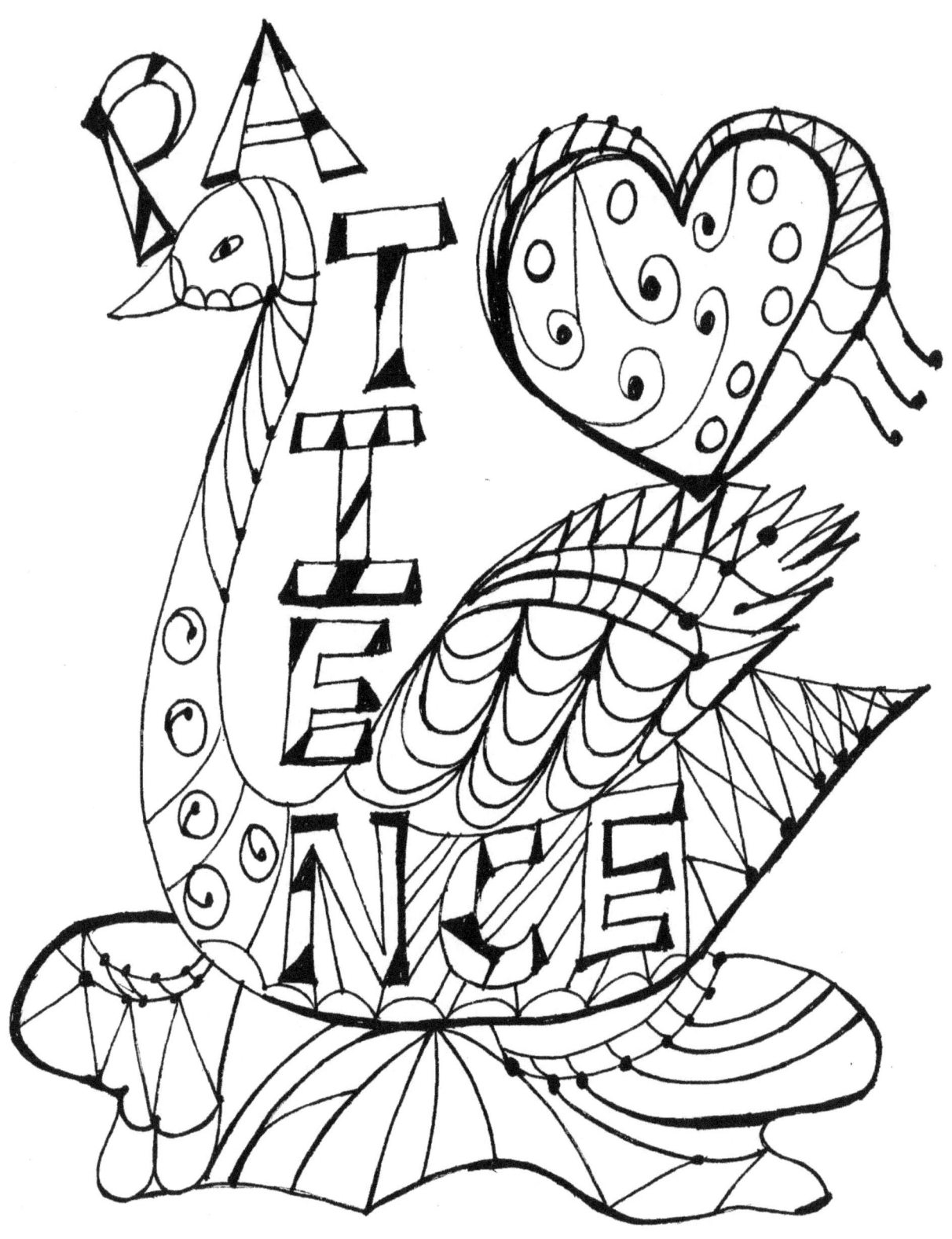

A friend loves at all times.

Proverbs 17:17

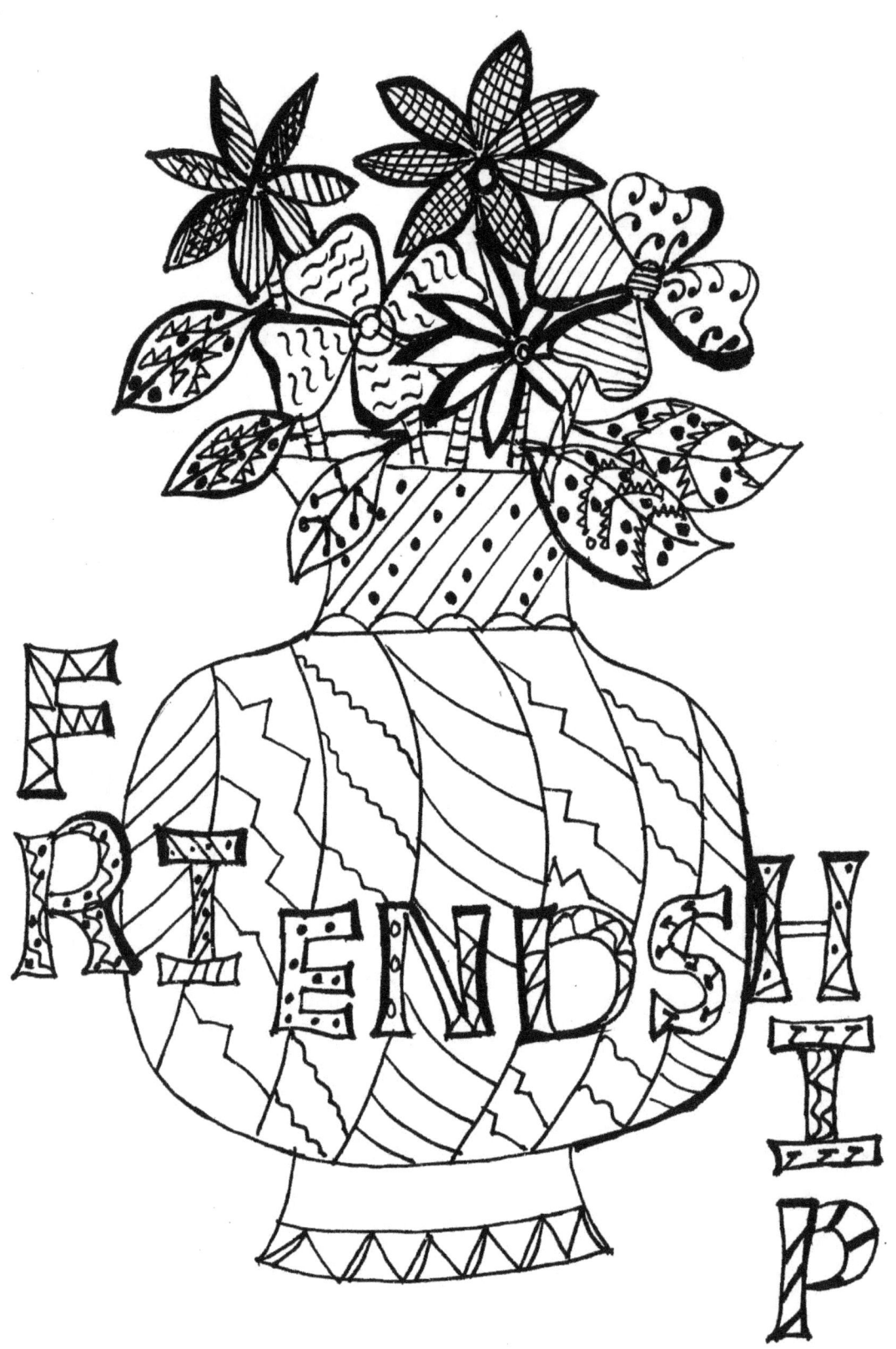

Make a joyful noise to the LORD.

Psalm 1:1

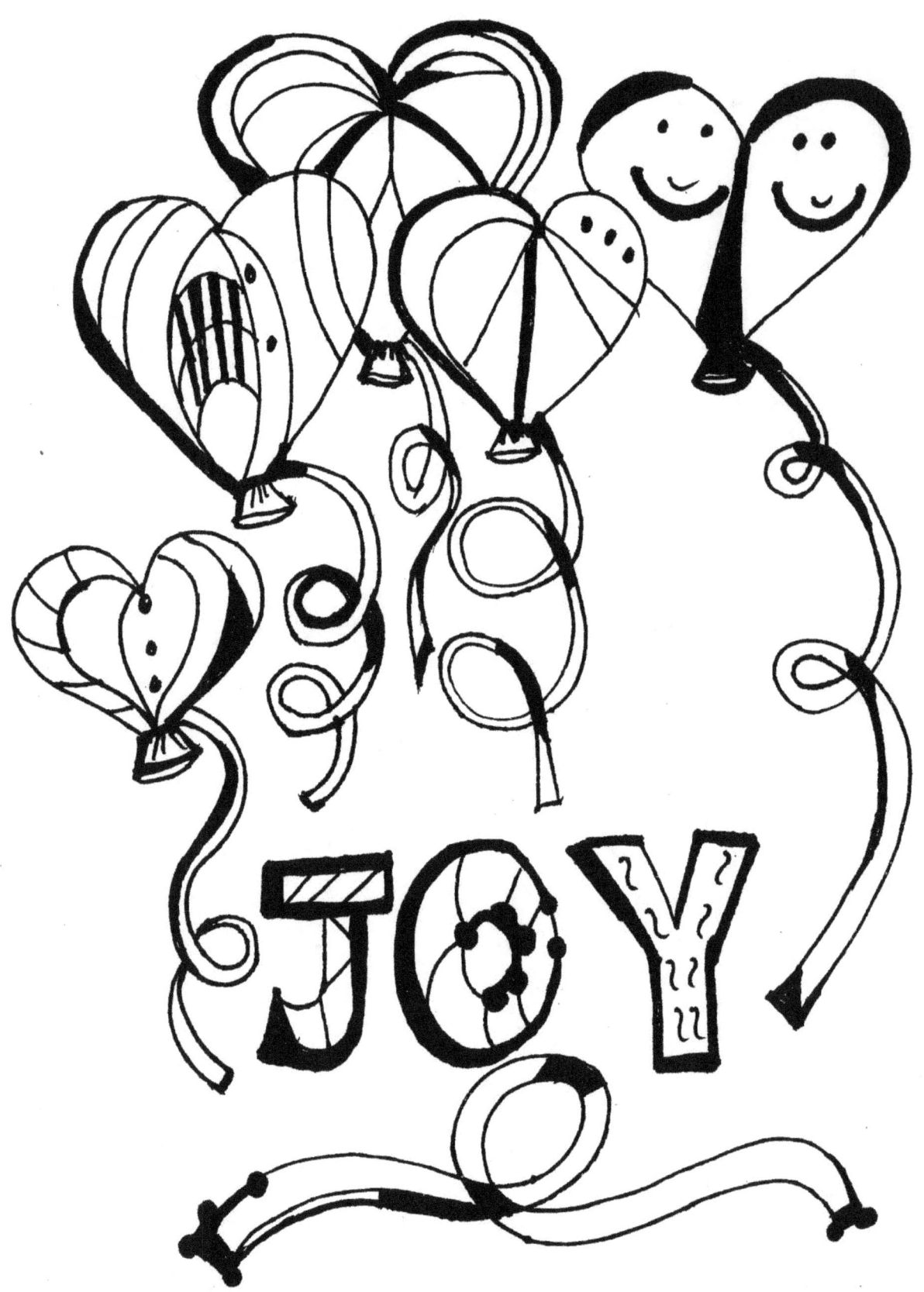

Humble yourself before the Lord, and he will lift you up.

James 4:10

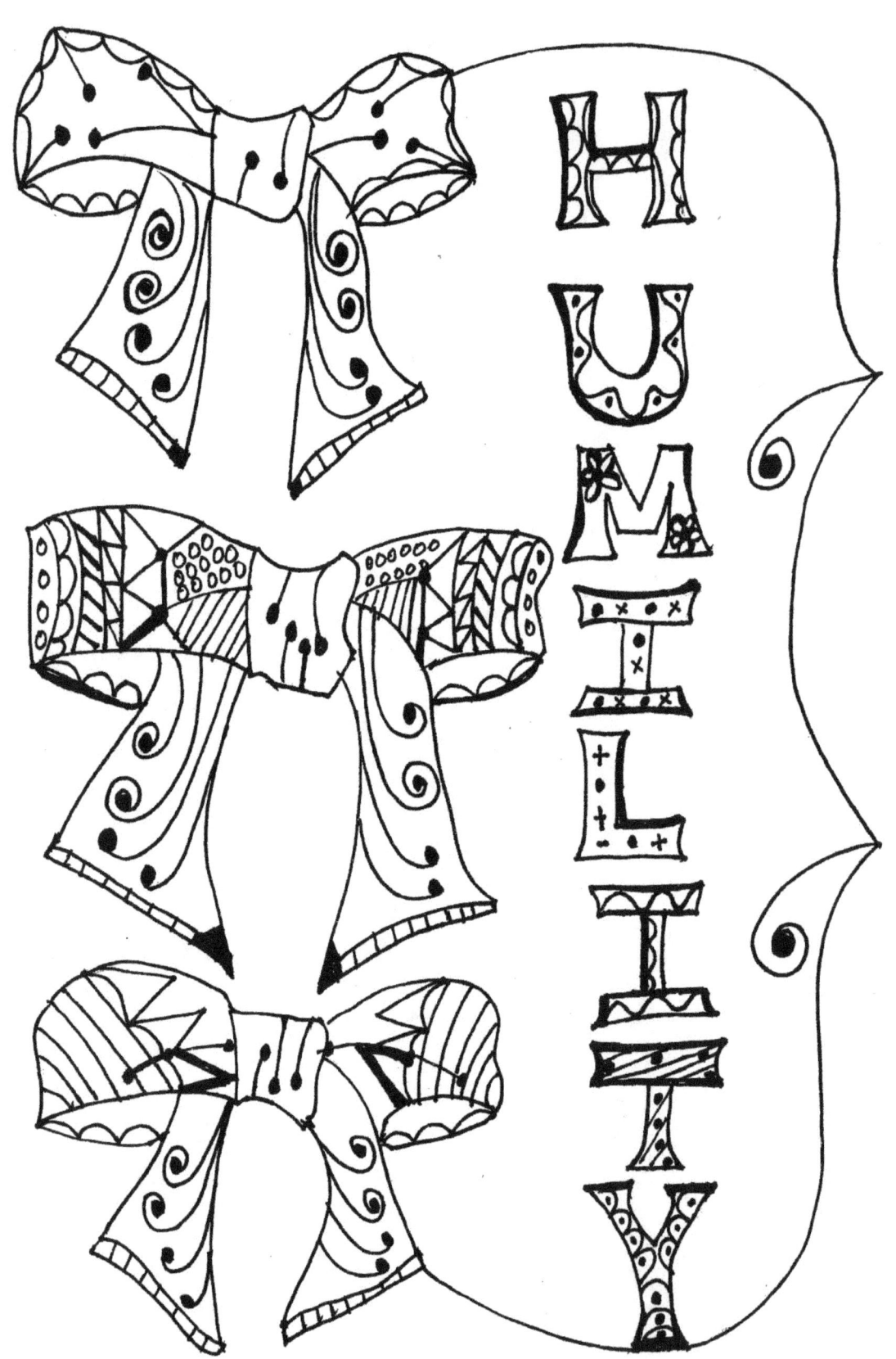

Without holiness no one will see the Lord.

Hebrews 12:14

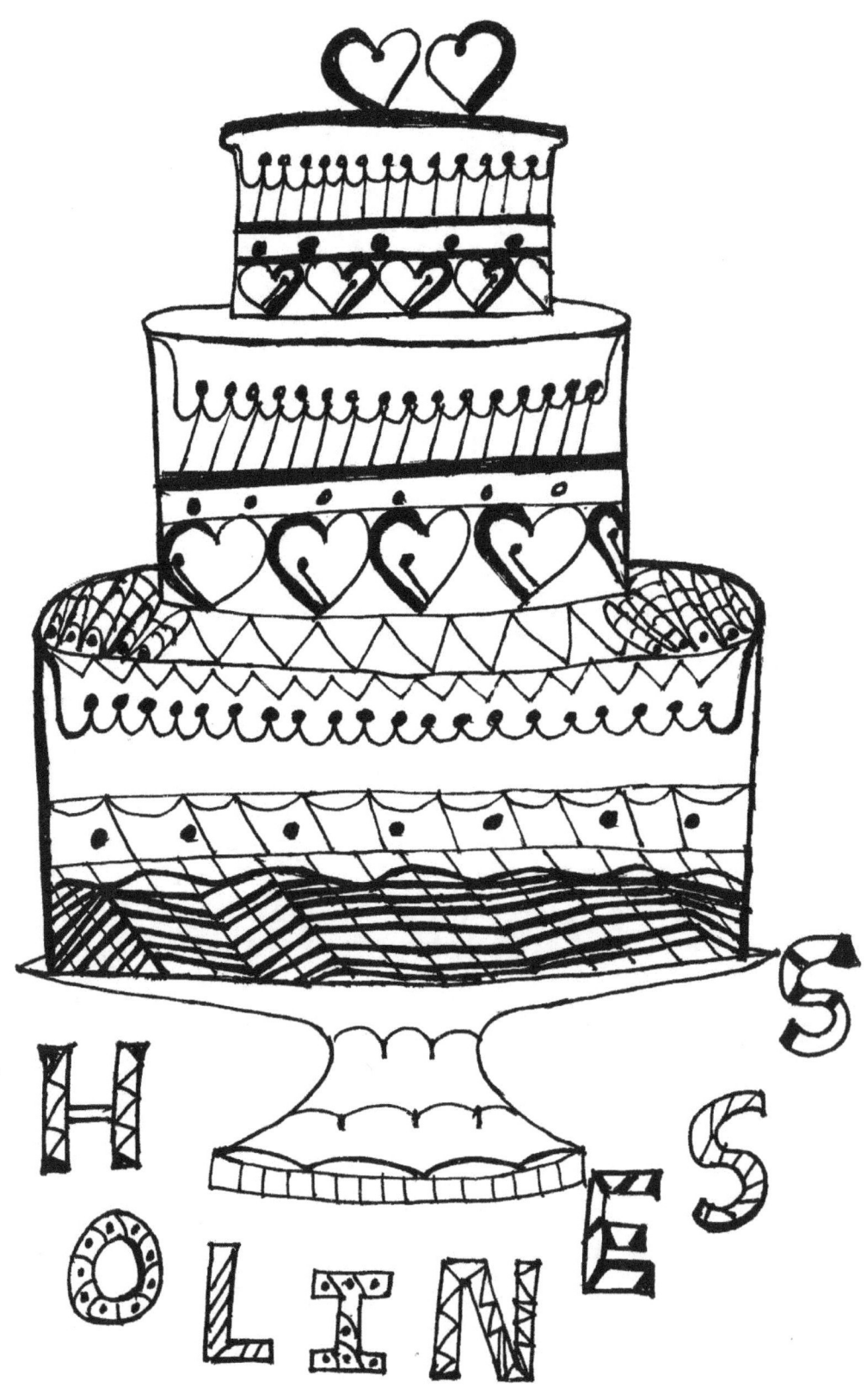

Other books by Simone Gillespie

Available On Amazon

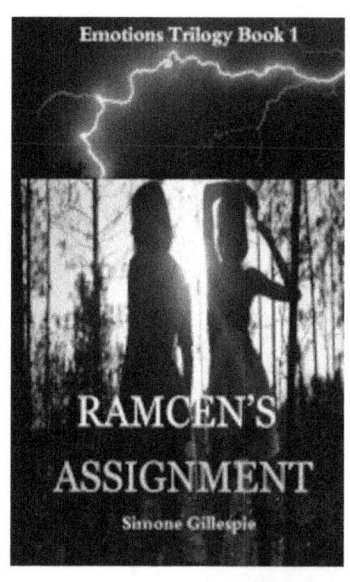

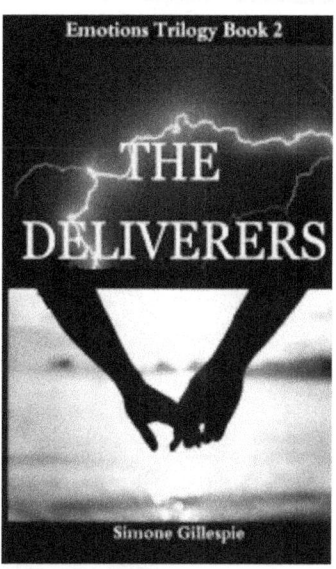

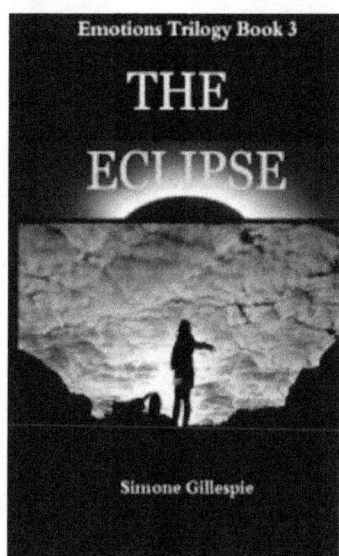

www.ingramcontent.com/pod-product-compliance
Lightning Source LLC
Chambersburg PA
CBHW080707190526
45169CB00006B/2282